To Liberty and Annabelle. May you spread your wings
but always find your way home. —J. S.

For Dad, who once rescued a sparrow after
it hit a glass window —B. P.

SIMON & SCHUSTER BOOKS FOR YOUNG READERS • An imprint of Simon & Schuster Children's Publishing Division • 1230 Avenue of the Americas, New York, New York 10020 • Text © 2024 by Jessica Stremer Illustration © 2024 by Bonnie Pang • Book design by Laura Eckes © 2024 by Simon & Schuster, Inc. • All rights reserved, including the right of reproduction in whole or in part in any form. • SIMON & SCHUSTER BOOKS FOR YOUNG READERS and related marks are trademarks of Simon & Schuster, Inc. • Simon & Schuster: Celebrating 100 Years of Publishing in 2024 • For information about special discounts for bulk purchases, please contact Simon & Schuster Special Sales at 1–866–506–1949 or business@simonandschuster.com. • The Simon & Schuster Speakers Bureau can bring authors to your live event. For more information or to book an event, contact the Simon & Schuster Speakers Bureau at 1–866–248–3049 or visit our website at www.simonspeakers.com. • The text for this book was set in The Cat's Whiskers. • The illustrations for this book were rendered digitally. • Manufactured in China • 1023 SCP • First Edition • 2   4   6   8   10   9   7   5   3   1 • Library of Congress Cataloging-in-Publication Data • Names: Stremer, Jessica, author I Pang, Bonnie, illustrator • Title: Lights out : a movement to help migrating birds / Jessica Stremer ; illustrated by Bonnie Pang. • Description: first edition. I New York : A Paula Wiseman Book, Simon & Schuster Books for Young Readers, 2024 I Includes bibliographical references. I Audience: Ages 4–8 I Audience: Grades 2–3 I Summary: "Based on the real-life Lights Out movement, this inspirational story shows how people can combat light pollution and make a big difference in helping to save migrating birds by turning lights off at night" –Provided by publisher. • Identifiers: LCCN 2023006373 (print) I LCCN 2023006374 (ebook) I ISBN 9781665931977 (hardcover) I ISBN 9781665931984 (ebook) • Subjects: LCSH: Migratory birds–Effect of light on–Juvenile literature. I Migratory birds–Conservation–Juvenile literature. • Classification: LCC QL698.9 .S77 2024 • (print) I LCC QL698.9 (ebook) I DDC 598.156/8–dc23/eng/20230424 • LC record available at https://lccn.loc.gov/2023006373 • LC ebook record available at https://lccn.loc.gov/2023006374

written by
JESSICA STREMER

illustrated by
BONNIE PANG

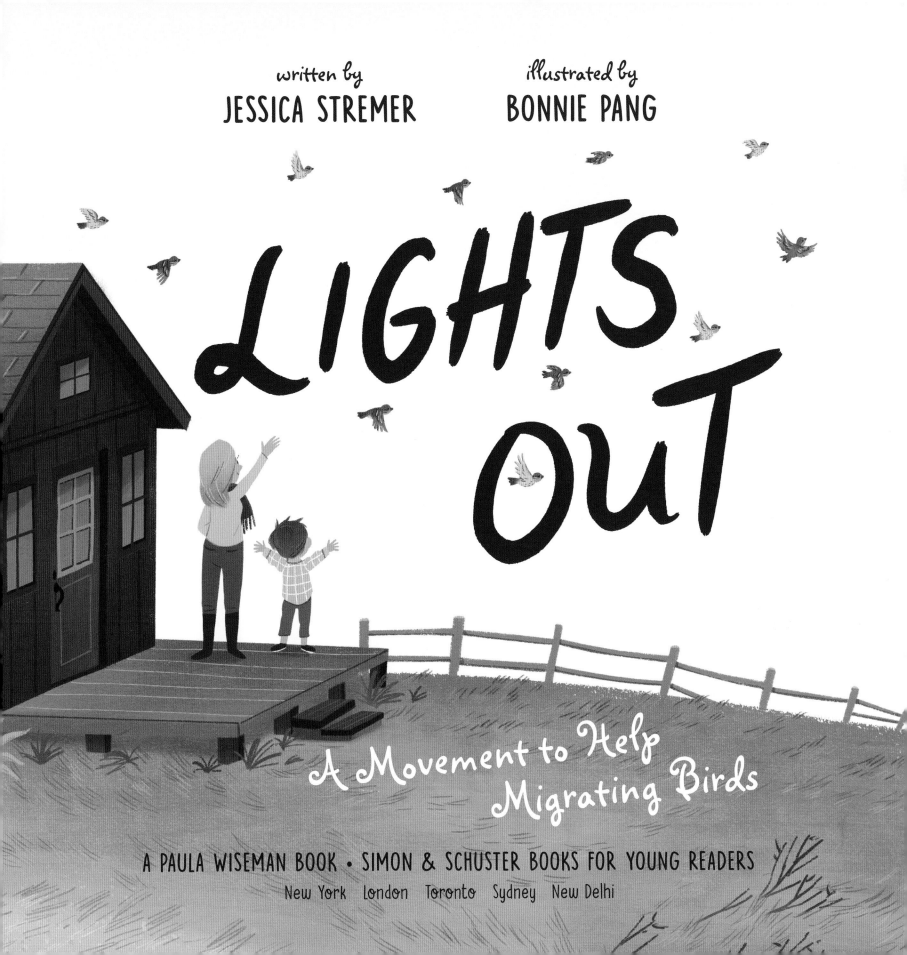

LIGHTS OUT

A Movement to Help Migrating Birds

A PAULA WISEMAN BOOK · SIMON & SCHUSTER BOOKS FOR YOUNG READERS
New York   London   Toronto   Sydney   New Delhi

When the air becomes cold
and the fields are bare,
a flock of sparrows know it's time to fly south for the winter.

Under the cover of darkness,
first one sparrow,
then many . . .

take flight!

A map made of stars guides them
over fields and forests.

But in the city,
headlights and billboards glare.
Business signs and streetlights shine.

The starry map disappears
as the dark sky is filled . . .

Confused, the sparrows fly
in the wrong direction,
toward the city.

Lost in the maze of windows
and blinding lights,
the sparrows search for a way
back to their starry map.

With scared chirps, they call out,

Here I am! Where are you?

But their calls bounce off buildings,

confusing the sparrows even more.

At long last, daylight returns.
One sparrow, then many,
find a way out of the city.

But one sparrow sits scared,

lost,

lonely,

left behind.

Until . . .

. . . helping hands scoop up the sparrow . . .

. . . and take it to a safe place.

"How can I help?" asks the girl.

The sparrow stays behind to
rest and heal,
but the girl leaves
with a plan.

First one child, then many, write letters
to neighbors,

business owners,
people all over the city.

Asking them to turn off their lights at night
so the birds can see the starry map.

The children paint posters
and draw pictures to hang in
windows so the birds don't
fly into the glass.

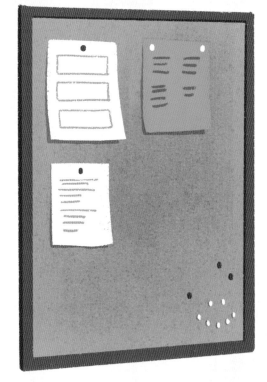

From city to city,
voices big and small cry out:

"*Save the sparrows!*"

The movement spreads like a bird's song carried by the wind.

But will the plan work?

When the weather changes,
the sparrows know it's time to
return north.

Under the cover of darkness,
first one sparrow,
then many,

take flight!

Only this time . . .

. . . all across the cities,
the lights . . .

. . . go out.

Stars twinkle like tiny bread crumbs, leading the way.

The left-behind sparrow,
now healed,
rejoins its flock . . .

. . . as they safely make
their way back home.

Birds, Migration, and the Dangers of Light Pollution

Birds play an important role in the world around us. They help spread seeds, pollinate plants, and eat pesky insects. Many birds, including sparrows, migrate thousands of miles in the spring and the fall in search of food and places to raise their young, and to escape the harsh weather.

To prepare for the long journey, they fill their bellies with seeds and insects, nearly doubling their body weight in the process.

Scientists believe birds use a combination of magnetism, stars, and natural landmarks to aid in navigation. About 80 percent of birds travel at night, when the sky is calmer and predators are less active.

Light pollution causes birds to become distracted and disoriented during migration. Some cities are more dangerous to birds than others, owing to a combination of the height of the buildings and weather patterns. Many cities located along popular migration routes are leading aggressive Lights Out campaigns to help provide a safer passage for birds.

But disorientation from light pollution isn't the only problem. Many birds get injured or die when they collide with windows. This confusion happens because birds are unable to tell the difference between actual plants and the reflections of plants they see in a window. Some species of birds, such as the song sparrows in this story, are considered "super colliders," in that they have a higher rate of dying from building collisions than other migratory birds. Researchers think this may be because they fly lower to the ground and their calls further add to their confusion.

More about Lights Out

In 1993 a small group of volunteers in Toronto, Ontario, created FLAP (Fatal Light Awareness Program) Canada. The idea came after volunteers noticed that bird collisions with lit buildings were greater than those with unlit ones.

FLAP Canada volunteers began asking business owners, especially those of tall buildings, to turn off all unnecessary lights during peak migration periods. At first many refused to participate. But as news stations reported on the bird collisions, teachers began mailing letters and drawings from their students. Even Prince Philip of the United Kingdom stepped up to help by offering to take a photograph with participants.

As more and more businesses agreed to participate, the success of the Lights Out campaign grew. Gradually, other birding organizations around the world learned about FLAP Canada's efforts and launched campaigns in their cities.

Today FLAP Canada and the National Audubon Society in the United States work with cities across North America to turn off unnecessary lights during peak migration seasons, and to encourage the construction of bird-friendly buildings.

How to Help

No matter where you live, you can take small actions to help migratory birds.

- Use migration maps such as the one found at birdcast.info to monitor migration activities in your area.

- Turn off all unnecessary outdoor lights, or replace them with lights that are bird-friendly, such as motion-activated lights or shielded luminaries that control glare.

- Write letters to city leaders and business owners asking them to join Lights Out.

- Make your windows safer for birds by placing a small sticker or decal on the outside of the window, covering the window with one-way transparent film, or installing screens specifically designed to protect birds.

- If you come across an injured bird, do not pick it up. Call your local wildlife control or Audubon Society, or ask an adult to use a towel or gloves to safely put the bird in a box to bring to a rehab center.

- Plant native trees and shrubs in your yard to offer birds additional food and shelter.

Flyways

Flyways are common routes birds use when migrating between winter and summer nesting areas. We can compare them to the highways we drive on to get from one location to another. Scientists monitor flyway habitats to learn more about migratory bird populations and behavior. Sometimes this involves putting a small band around a bird's ankle to track its movement year after year. Radar is also used to detect and map when and where large numbers of birds are flying. Scientists can use this information to predict migration patterns and inform people of recommended periods of lights-out.

Bibliography

American Bird Conservancy. "Threats." Accessed January 21, 2021. https://abcbirds.org/threats/.

eBird. "Song Sparrow." Accessed September 20, 2022. https://ebird.org/species/sonspa.

FLAP Canada. "Home." Accessed September 20, 2022. https://flap.org/.

FLAP Canada. "Solutions for Commercial and Institutional Buildings." Accessed September 20, 2022.
    https://flap.org/solutions-commercial-institutional/.

International Dark-Sky Association. "Light Pollution Effects on Wildlife and Ecosystems." Accessed September 20, 2022.
    https://www.darksky.org/light-pollution/wildlife/.

Lockhart, Jhaneel. "9 Awesome Facts about Bird Migration." National Audubon Society. October 11, 2012.
    https://www.audubon.org/news/9-awesome-facts-about-bird-migration.

National Audubon Society. "Bird-Friendly Buildings." Accessed September 20, 2022.
    https://www.audubon.org/bird-friendly-buildings.

National Audubon Society. "Flyways of the Americas." Accessed June 27, 2022. https://www.audubon.org/birds/flyways.

National Audubon Society. "Lights Out." Accessed September 20, 2022. http://www.audubon.org/lights-out-program.

Old Bird. "Home." Accessed September 20, 2022. http://oldbird.org/index2.htm.

Yeoman, Barry. "What Do Birds Do for Us?" National Audubon Society. April 8, 2013. https://www.audubon.org/news
    /what-do-birds-do-us#:~:text=Pest%20control%2C%20public%20health%2C%20seed,the%20ways%20birds%20
    benefit%20humans.

Acknowledgments

I'd like to thank Michael Mesure, executive director and
cofounder of FLAP Canada, and Robyn Coole, wildlife
biologist, for their efforts to protect our feathered
friends and for verifying the accuracy of
the information presented in this book.